JAZZIN' ABOUT
fun pieces for
FLUTE

CONTENTS

PAM WEDGWOOD

FABER ff MUSIC

TO THE TEACHER

Jazzin' About is an original collection of material written in popular Rock and Jazz styles.

The pieces are arranged approximately in order of increasing difficulty and I hope that teachers will find this collection a useful addition to any teaching programme, providing a firm foundation for more advanced studies in this style of playing. Stimulating accompaniments for piano (or electric/electronic keyboard) will help the student to achieve scrupulous articulation of rhythmic patterns and familiarity with the feeling and characteristics of the music.

One of the most important aspects of teaching a musical instrument is to ensure that the student enjoys what he or she plays. The study of varied idioms will encourage the pupil to progress faster both technically and musically.

TO THE STUDENT

My primary reason for writing **Jazzin' About** is to give you an opportunity to play in popular styles while you are in the earlier stages of your musical development. Jazz, Rock and Blues are all part of our musical heritage and should be experienced along with more 'classically' orientated works. However, learning to master popular rhythms can be hard work as well as fun! Once you have learnt each phrase, try to put a little of your own expression and style into it. Persuade your friends to join in!

I hope that **Jazzin' About** will give you new satisfaction and enthusiasm for your instrument.

Happy Blowing!

Pamela Wedgwood.

© 1992 by Faber Music Ltd
First published in 1992 by Faber Music Ltd
3 Queen Square London WC1N 3AU
Cover by velladesign
Music engraved by Seton Music Graphics
Printed in England by Caligraving Ltd

ISBN 0-571-51275-5

To buy Faber Music publications or to find out about the full range of titles available please contact your local music retailer or Faber Music sales enquiries:

Faber Music Limited, Burnt Mill, Elizabeth Way, Harlow, CM20 2HX England
Tel: +44 (0)1279 82 89 82   Fax: +44 (0)1279 82 89 83
sales@fabermusic.com   www.fabermusic.com

1. Hot on the Line

PAMELA WEDGWOOD

2. Pink Lady

Lyrical, with movement (♩=126)

8

3. Free Fall

4. Going Home

5. Ho Down - Show Down

6. Just Passing By

7. Out of Nowhere

8. Tequila Sunrise

D.C. al ⊕ poi al Coda

CODA

The JAZZIN' ABOUT Series

PAM WEDGWOOD

Christmas Jazzin' About. Piano	ISBN 0-571-51507-X
Christmas Jazzin' About. Piano Duet	ISBN 0-571-51584-3
Christmas Jazzin' About. Violin	ISBN 0-571-51694-7
Christmas Jazzin' About. Cello	ISBN 0-571-51695-5
Christmas Jazzin' About. Flute	ISBN 0-571-51586-X
Christmas Jazzin' About. Clarinet	ISBN 0-571-51585-1
Christmas Jazzin' About. Alto Saxophone	ISBN 0-571-51587-8
Christmas Jazzin' About. Trumpet	ISBN 0-571-51696-3
Easy Jazzin' About. Piano	ISBN 0-571-51337-9
Easy Jazzin' About. Piano Duets	ISBN 0-571-51661-0
Green Jazzin' About. Piano	ISBN 0-571-51645-9
Jazzin' About. Piano	ISBN 0-571-51105-8
Jazzin' About. Piano Duets	ISBN 0-571-51662-9
Jazzin' About. Violin	ISBN 0-571-51315-8
Jazzin' About. Cello	ISBN 0-571-51316-6
Jazzin' About. Flute	ISBN 0-571-51275-5
Jazzin' About. Clarinet	ISBN 0-571-51273-9
Jazzin' About. Alto Saxophone	ISBN 0-571-51054-X
Jazzin' About. Trumpet	ISBN 0-571-51039-6
Jazzin' About. Trombone	ISBN 0-571-51053-1
Jazzin' About Styles. Piano	ISBN 0-571-51718-8
More Jazzin' About. Piano	ISBN 0-571-51437-5
Really Easy Jazzin' About. Piano	ISBN 0-571-52089-8

FABER ff MUSIC